Original title:
Jasmine Motifs Among the Unicorn Nest

Author: Lan Donne
ISBN HARDBACK: 978-1-80562-654-1
ISBN PAPERBACK: 978-1-80564-175-9

Vibrant Secrets Amidst the Celestial Grove

In shadows deep where whispers dwell,
The ancient trees their secrets tell.
With emerald leaves that dance and sway,
They guard the night, the fading day.

Beneath the stars that twinkle bright,
A tapestry of soft moonlight.
The air is laced with magic sweet,
Where dreams and twilight softly meet.

Each fluttering leaf, a tale untold,
Of wanderers brave and treasures bold.
The secrets of the grove align,
In nature's rhythm, pure and divine.

So heed the call of the nightingale,
And listen close to the heart's soft trail.
Among the roots, old wisdom flows,
In vibrant hues, the forest grows.

Embrace the whispers, hold them dear,
For in the grove, our dreams draw near.
With every breath, let wonder bloom,
In this celestial, sacred room.

Times of Enchantment and Fragrance

In the twilight of the enchanted hours,
When the air is filled with blooming flowers,
The fragrance drifts on gentle sighs,
Carrying whispers from starlit skies.

Every moment wrapped in delight,
Magic lingers, both day and night.
The scent of jasmine fills the air,
Inviting dreams beyond compare.

Underneath the willow's weeping bough,
Time seems to pause and gently bow.
The spirits of nature softly hum,
To the rhythm of where fairies come.

In such times, hearts open wide,
To the wonders unfolding outside.
With every breeze, enchantment calls,
As twilight blushes and softly falls.

So cherish the magic in every breath,
In these moments that dance toward death.
For in the fragrance, dreams reside,
As time drifts gently like the tide.

Ethereal Petals in Soothing Breezes

In the meadow, where soft winds play,
Ethereal petals in colors sway.
They catch the light, a delicate gleam,
Whispering secrets of a waking dream.

The breeze, a lullaby on the skin,
Brings tales of warmth from deep within.
As dandelions float in a gentle stream,
Carrying wishes where hearts can beam.

Nature's brush paints with tender care,
Each hue a promise, beyond compare.
From violet dusk to azure dawn,
Life awakens, worries withdrawn.

The dance of petals, a soothing song,
Reminding us where our souls belong.
In the stillness of twilight's grace,
We find our place in nature's embrace.

So linger awhile in this serene space,
Let the world vanish without a trace.
For in ethereal presence, love is found,
In soothing breezes and beauty unbound.

Timeless Beauty in Fantasy Gardens

In gardens where the whispers play,
The petals dance in soft array.
With every breeze, a tale unfolds,
Of magic lost and treasures told.

The sunlight spills like golden wine,
Upon the paths where wonders shine.
Each bloom a story, bright and rare,
In timeless hues beyond compare.

With lilac dreams and roses bold,
Their secrets, sweet as days of old.
The fragrance lingers, soft and light,
A spell beneath the starry night.

In shadows deep where fairies tread,
The seeds of hope and love are spread.
Each leaf a promise, brave and true,
Reminds us of a world anew.

So wander through this vibrant space,
Where every turn, a warm embrace.
In fantasy, we find our way,
In gardens where our hearts can play.

The Allure of Petal-Woven Myths

In glades where petal-woven myths,
Are cradled tight, like cherished gifts.
Each bloom a word in ancient lore,
That whispers tales forevermore.

The morning dew, like silver tears,
Reflects the joys of yesteryears.
With shimmering lights that softly glide,
Through memories that time can't hide.

The winds of change do sweep the earth,
Yet in these blossoms lingers mirth.
A tapestry of colors bright,
That dances gently in the light.

With every step upon this trail,
The heart begins to weave a tale.
Of knights and dragons, love's embrace,
In gardens filled with sacred grace.

So let us wander, hand in hand,
Through stories spun in petal-land.
The allure of myths awaits us there,
In fragrant blooms beyond compare.

Fantasia Under Canopies of Bloom

Beneath the arches, dreams take flight,
Where blossoms gather, bold and bright.
A symphony of colors call,
In fantastical embrace for all.

The lilting notes of nature's song,
In canopies where hearts belong.
With every rustle, every sigh,
The world transforms, both low and high.

In twilight's glow, the petals gleam,
Awakening the tender dream.
A gentle hush, the stars ascend,
As night descends, our souls commend.

So here we'll craft our secret space,
In every leaf, a warm embrace.
With whispered tales in shadows cast,
We find our peace, our hearts steadfast.

Here in this land, wild and free,
We gather gifts of mystery.
Fantasia lives while flowers bloom,
A cherished spell that breaks the gloom.

Serenades of Light and Flora

In mornings kissed by dewy light,
The world awakens, pure delight.
With flows of color, bright and bold,
Each petal sings of tales retold.

Serenades of flora float,
On gentle winds, a fairy's note.
With every stem and vibrant hue,
The heart embraces something new.

As shadows dance in twilight's hold,
The gospel of the blooms unfolds.
Their secrets buried deep in earth,
Do whisper soft of love and mirth.

In gardens rich, we seek the muse,
In fragrant notes, we cannot lose.
With every breeze, our souls take wing,
To write the songs that flowers sing.

So come, dear friend, and share this sight,
Where every corner holds delight.
In serenades of light and flora,
We find a world, forever more-a.

Nocturnal Fragrance of Twilight Tales

In twilight's breath, the flowers sigh,
A whisper of dreams as night drifts by.
The moonlight weaves a silver thread,
Among the petals, where secrets spread.

Stars awaken in the violet hue,
Shadows dance where the cool winds blew.
Each scent a story, old and wise,
Beneath the watchful, starry skies.

Night's gentle hand paints colors bright,
With strokes of whisper and soft delight.
Crickets sing, the owls reply,
As magic lingers, time drifts high.

Every breeze carries a lore anew,
Of lovers lost and sorrows too.
In fragrant tales, the heart will dwell,
Where twilight weaves its timeless spell.

So let us wander through this night,
With fragrant dreams that take to flight.
In every blossom, a light unfolds,
A journey woven in dusk's soft folds.

Chasing Shadows in a Flowered Grove

In the grove where wildflowers bloom,
Shadows flicker, dispelling gloom.
The sunbeams play on the emerald leaves,
Where laughter hides and the heart believes.

Petals flutter in the gentle breeze,
Whispers echo through ancient trees.
Each stroll unveils a hidden path,
As nature's magic fuels our laugh.

Through twisted vines, we chase the light,
Dancing shadows, a playful flight.
In fragrant air, the stories grow,
Of dreams and wishes we once sowed.

Beneath the canopy of dappled shade,
Memories linger, never to fade.
In every corner, a secret glows,
While the flowered grove, its beauty shows.

So let us chase till the day is done,
Through wildflower fields, in joyful run.
For in this place where shadows blend,
We find our hearts, where the magic bends.

The Grace of Legends Intertwined

In whispered tales of times long past,
Legends flutter like shadows cast.
Echoes linger in the twilight air,
With every heartbeat, stories share.

From ancient woods where spirits soar,
To misty moors and forgotten lore.
Graceful figures dance in the dusk,
Their laughter mingles, sweet and husk.

Through tangled roots and winding streams,
We trace the paths of faded dreams.
Each step we take, a tale unfurls,
Of knights and creatures, enchanted worlds.

In moonlit nights, where secrets weave,
The grace of legends we believe.
With every glance, the past aligns,
In timeless beauty, love entwines.

So sit with me by the fireside bright,
As shadows whisper of long-lost night.
Together we'll weave a tapestry,
Of all the legends that came to be.

Harmonies of Nature's Crown

In every leaf, a song is found,
The gentle rustle, a blissful sound.
From mountain high to river's bend,
Nature's chorus will never end.

The babbling brook hums a tune,
While crickets serenade the moon.
Each note sung, a spirit free,
A dance of life, in harmony.

In fields where wildflowers sway and twirl,
Colors burst forth, a vibrant whirl.
With buzzing bees and birds in flight,
Nature's palette paints pure delight.

The wind carries whispers through the trees,
A symphony played by the gentle breeze.
Each harmony, both fierce and soft,
Reminds us of the magic aloft.

So let's embrace this sweet refrain,
As nature's beauty sings our gain.
In every heart, let the music dwell,
The harmonies of life cast their spell.

Meadow Serenades with Celestial Creatures

In meadows green, where fairies play,
With laughter light, and dreams at bay.
Beneath the clouds, they twirl and spin,
Each whispered song a tale to win.

The daisies dance, in sparkling hues,
While moonlit beams cast gentle views.
A shimmering mist leads the way,
To hidden realms where night meets day.

With twinkling stars that wink and glow,
Celestial friends in twilight flow.
They weave their magic through the night,
A melody of pure delight.

Amidst the blooms, the fireflies wink,
In secret glades, their fates in sync.
With every flit, a story shared,
Of brave new worlds and dreams prepared.

So linger long in nature's grace,
Find joy in every enchanted space.
For in the meadows, dreams take flight,
With celestial creatures, pure and bright.

Whispers of Radiance in Floral Tales

In gardens vast, where colors merge,
The blooms awake, the breezes surge.
With petals soft and stems so tall,
They whisper secrets through it all.

A tale of sun, of rain, of glee,
Each flower sings of mystery.
The roses blush as zephyrs tease,
While lilies sway in silent ease.

Bright daffodils, with golden cheer,
Unfurl their hearts as spring draws near.
Their laughter rings, a joyful sound,
In every corner, magic found.

The violets nod, with heads held high,
They catch the glance of passing sky.
In floral realms where spirits dance,
Each bloom invites a fleeting chance.

So breathe the fragrance, let it stay,
As whispers weave throughout the day.
In floral tales of light and shade,
The beauty blooms, and dreams are made.

Unfurling Petals of Whimsy and Wonder

With blushing buds that greet the morn,
Each petal speaks where dreams are born.
In gardens where the wild hearts dwell,
Whimsy thrives, enchanting well.

The tulips twirl in vibrant arcs,
Inviting joy with whispered sparks.
Through archways green, the breezes play,
As wonder weaves the light of day.

A butterfly, in colors bright,
Unfurls its wings, takes to the light.
It flits from bloom to bloom with grace,
In this magical, sacred space.

The daisies wink with gentle pride,
As secrets of the sky confide.
Each wandering spirit finds their way,
In petals soft that come to stay.

So let your heart, like flowers, bloom,
In every shadow, chase the gloom.
For whimsy grows where wonder roams,
In nature's plant, we find our homes.

Echoes of Magic Beneath Flowered Canopies

Beneath the boughs where blossoms cling,
The echoes play of tales we sing.
In shades of green, where shadows dance,
The heart is lost in every glance.

As twilight drapes its velvet shroud,
The blooms awaken, bright and proud.
With each soft rustle, secrets swell,
Of worlds where fairies dwell and tell.

The garden hums, enchantment weaves,
In every rustling, nature breathes.
With flowered canopies that sway,
The magic blooms, and dreams convey.

Among the petals, whispers twine,
In fragrant notes, their fates align.
A symphony of life unfolds,
In echoes soft, the story holds.

So roam beneath the jeweled skies,
Where every moment gives a gift of sighs.
For in the flowered halls they dwell,
Magic lingers, casting its spell.

Whispers of Enchanted Blooms

In gardens where the fairies dwell,
Each blossom holds a magic spell.
Their colors dance in gentle light,
A symphony of pure delight.

The winds do carry secrets fair,
Of tales spun in the fragrant air.
Petals whisper, twirl, and sway,
Inviting dreams to drift away.

With every dew-kissed leaf unfurled,
A story waits to be unhurled.
A bond of nature, strong and true,
The blooms, they know it all anew.

Amongst the roots, a world unknown,
Where whispered wishes lie alone.
The magic breathes, alive and bright,
In shadows cast by fading light.

So pause awhile, let time stand still,
In gardens where the heart can fill.
With whispers soft of love and grace,
In every bloom, a warm embrace.

Velvet Petals in Moonlight

Beneath a sky of silken dreams,
The garden glows with silver beams.
Velvet petals softly glow,
While secrets sway, and starlight flows.

The night unfolds its gentle arms,
Embracing all with timeless charms.
Each flower breathes a silent tune,
Beneath the gaze of watchful moon.

With every breeze, a story stirs,
As time is caught in gentle whirs.
The magic hums through fragrant air,
A dance of shadows everywhere.

In dreams, the blossoms start to twine,
As moonbeams weave a soft design.
The garden whispers in delight,
Embracing all who roam its night.

So linger in this world divine,
Where velvet petals intertwine.
The night unveils its mystery,
In moonlit blooms, pure ecstasy.

Celestial Dreams in Floral Realms

In realms where flowers touch the stars,
Dreams are scattered near and far.
A tapestry of color bright,
Awaits the heart in endless flight.

Each petal glimmers with a glow,
Unfolding tales of long ago.
Celestial whispers fill the air,
Entwining hopes with gentle care.

With every bloom, a wish takes flight,
Into the vast and endless night.
A fragrant breeze, a soft refrain,
Where dreams make roots, then grow again.

The stars peer down with twinkling eyes,
To witness all the heart's replies.
A garden lush where magic thrives,
In floral realms, our spirit dives.

So chase the dawn, let sunlight beam,
Awake anew within the dream.
For in this land of blooms galore,
Celestial wonders hum and soar.

The Secret Garden of Mythical Beasts

Where shadows dwell and whispers creep,
The secret garden, safely deep.
With wings of gold and scales of dreams,
Mythical beasts guard flowing streams.

In twilight hour, they softly roam,
In search of shadows they call home.
Each flower blooms with daring grace,
A haven forged in time and space.

From leafy boughs, the magic hums,
As ancient lore in silence drums.
A unicorn prances through the glade,
While faeries weave a silver braid.

The roses blush with secrets bold,
Of legends lost and tales retold.
In every petal, myths entwine,
As beasts and blooms in splendor shine.

So wander through this world of dreams,
Where magic flows in bright moonbeams.
A garden filled with heart and art,
Where mythical wonders never part.

Dreams Drifting on a Floral Breeze

In gardens where the wild winds play,
The dreams take flight on softest day.
With whispers sweet, the petals sway,
And jasmine scents the twilight's gray.

Beneath the arch of twilight's gleam,
The stars awaken, softly beam.
Each flicker tells of hopes and schemes,
As shadows dance in moonlit dream.

A butterfly, with wings so bright,
Glides through the veils of silver light.
It carries wishes, pure and slight,
To realms where hearts can take their flight.

And as the evening drapes its cloak,
The flowers whisper, gently spoke.
In fragrant breaths, the night awoke,
With tales of magic, lightly broke.

So let us linger, hearts entwined,
In gardens where the stars aligned.
With every petal, love designed,
The dreams we seek, forever bind.

The Ethereal Realm of Blooming Creatures

In whispering woods where secrets bloom,
The creatures dwell in twilight's gloom.
Each leaf a tale, each petal's plume,
Awakens magic, dispels the doom.

A fox with fur like autumn's fire,
Dances beneath the moon's attire.
With every leap, it sings of desire,
For dreams that lift us ever higher.

The rabbits, wise with silvered grace,
Gather beneath the ancient space.
Their eyes reflect the stars' embrace,
In nature's dance, we find our place.

A hummingbird, so swift and bright,
Flits through the blossoms, pure delight.
It carries joy on wings of light,
In every sip, a heart takes flight.

Thus in this realm where wonders tread,
The blooming creatures gently spread
Their tales of love, where dreams are fed,
And magic sings through all that's said.

Wildflowers and Legends Beneath the Stars

Wildflowers dance in fields so wide,
Where legends weave on twilight's tide.
Beneath the stars, our dreams abide,
In nature's hold, we take our stride.

The nightingale sings of yesteryears,
Of lost romances, hopes, and fears.
Its melody draws out the tears,
And in our hearts, the joy appears.

Each petal holds a story true,
Of whispered wishes, skies so blue.
They sway together, one and two,
Embracing love in every hue.

The moonlight spills upon the ground,
Illuminating dreams unbound.
With every sweet, enchanted sound,
We find the magic all around.

So let us tread on dewy grass,
Where wildflowers in beauty pass.
In this domain, where shadows cast,
We forge our legends, love amassed.

Tales of Nature's Enchanted Heart

In whispers soft, the forest calls,
With ancient trees that guard the falls.
Each step within, the magic sprawls,
As nature weaves its mystic thralls.

The brook sings stories, clear and bright,
Of woodland creatures and their flight.
In every ripple, pure delight,
Reflecting stars that kiss the night.

A doe appears, so calm and wise,
With gentle eyes like summer skies.
It teaches us to see the prize,
In silent moments, soft replies.

As greenery wraps the heart in care,
Each breath of wind becomes a prayer.
In nature's arms, we find our share,
Of timeless tales beyond compare.

So let us wander through this grace,
In every thicket, find our place.
For in this land of warm embrace,
We find the heart of nature's face.

Whispers of Enchanted Blossoms

In moonlit glades where shadows play,
The blossoms sway in soft ballet.
With secrets whispered on the breeze,
They dance beneath the ancient trees.

Each petal glows like dreams untold,
In hues of pink and threads of gold.
They sing of tales from long ago,
Of magic hid where few may go.

A breeze will stir the heart's delight,
As stars ignite the velvet night.
In every blush, a story's spun,
Of midnight magic and of fun.

The fragrance teases, calls to mind,
A world of wonder, sweet, aligned.
Where every bloom can softly speak,
And every lover's heart they seek.

So wander deep, where few have trod,
Embrace the mysteries, by God!
For in these whispers, life's enchant,
Awaits the brave, the bold, the grand.

Secrets in the Unicorn Meadow

In fields where dreams and stardust blend,
The unicorns in silence wend.
With hooves that touch the dewy grass,
They roam as shadows softly pass.

Each secret held in gentle heart,
Of magic's grace, a fragile art.
Their manes a swirl of silver light,
Illuminate the darkest night.

In whispers shared, they softly weave,
The tales of those who pause and believe.
A blessing felt in every sigh,
As wishes soar to the velvet sky.

Where flowers bloom in vibrant hues,
And morning dew awakes the muse,
The magic stirs in every breath,
A dance of life that conquers death.

So seek the glades where they abide,
With open hearts, and eyes so wide.
In every step, you'll feel the pull,
Of ancient spells, both kind and full.

The Elegance of Celestial Blooms

In gardens kissed by starlit trails,
Where twilight whispers secrets veils.
The blooms of night, so rare and bright,
Adorn the world in pure delight.

Like wishes spread in softest hue,
These flowers dance, both brave and true.
Their petals draped in silken sheen,
Each one a glimpse of what's unseen.

The gentle rustle calls to thee,
To join the night's sweet revelry.
With every breath, the magic stirs,
In harmony, the heart confers.

As moonlight casts a silver glow,
The garden blooms, a mystic show.
Each fragrance rich, a tale unfurled,
Of dreams that wander 'round the world.

So linger long in balmy air,
And touch the blooms that spin with care.
For in their elegance, you'll find,
A glimpse of love, both pure and blind.

Velvet Petals of Mythical Creatures

In twilight realms where magic brews,
The velvet petals catch the views.
In colors bright, they softly glow,
With stories waiting just to flow.

The creatures swirl in playful dance,
As petals twirl in sweet romance.
Each whisper floats on evening's sigh,
As hidden wonders flit and fly.

With gentle hands, the petals trace,
The outlines of a mystic place.
Where every bloom holds tales of old,
Of heart's desire and love so bold.

Among the ferns and silver streams,
Lie creatures born from starlit dreams.
They greet the night with laughter bright,
As velvet fades to morning light.

So wander deep in lands unseen,
Where every leaf is evergreen.
In mythical embrace, be whole,
With velvet petals weaving soul.

Echoes of Flora in the Realm of Dreams

In the garden where shadows play,
Whispering petals weave the day.
Gentle breezes softly hum,
Echoes of flora, calling, come.

Moonlit blossoms twinkle bright,
Dancing softly, pure delight.
In the realm where dreams entwine,
Nature's secrets, sweet divine.

Stars reflect on silver streams,
Carrying the weight of dreams.
Each fragrance tells a tale anew,
In the night, a magic brew.

Petal-paved paths lead the way,
To a world where spirits sway.
Nightingales sing lullabies,
Underneath the velvet skies.

As dawn arrives, the echoes fade,
In the light, new plans are laid.
Yet in hearts, the garden stays,
Forever tangled in its ways.

Garden of Radiant Enigma

Hidden deep where wonders bloom,
A garden weaves a fragrant loom.
Mysteries in colors bright,
Holding secrets out of sight.

Petals whisper in the breeze,
Tales of love among the trees.
Each bloom a story to unfold,
A radiant enigma to behold.

Luminous glow of twilight's kiss,
In this realm, there's endless bliss.
In every corner, shadows dance,
Inviting hearts to take a chance.

Butterflies in graceful flight,
Dazzle with their pure delight.
Nature's palette, vivid, rare,
A tapestry beyond compare.

In the silence, laughter plays,
In the garden's warm embrace stays.
With every dusk, the peace remains,
As the heart's longing still reigns.

The Amulet of Petals and Legends

Once, in a glade where magic sleeps,
An amulet hid where the willow weeps.
Crafted from petals of blooms so rare,
Holding the legends, secrets to share.

Ancient voices call from the past,
Whispering tales of love that lasts.
In twilight's glow, the stories wake,
Every heartbeat, a promise to make.

Looming shadows, a flicker, a tease,
Every rustle in the leafy trees.
Guarded fiercely by time and fate,
The amulet waits, a quiet gate.

Legends entwine with the roots so deep,
Harboring dreams that the ancients keep.
In a world where wishes fly,
It glimmers bright under the sky.

To hold the amulet is to believe,
In the tales that nature weaves.
With each petal, a story's told,
In the heart where magic unfolds.

Celestial Enchantment in Serene Spaces

Under stars, the universe sighs,
Celestial wonders fill the skies.
In serene spaces, peace resides,
Magic flows where heart abides.

Moonbeams dance on silver streams,
Weaving softly through our dreams.
Galaxies breathe an ancient tune,
As night unfolds beneath the moon.

Whispers echo in the night air,
Carried gently, a loving prayer.
Each twinkle tells a tale profound,
In the velvet dark, miracles abound.

Floating lanterns of hope ignite,
Illuminating the realms of night.
With every flicker, hearts take flight,
Capturing dreams, a wondrous sight.

Embrace the enchantment, let it grow,
In serene spaces, the magic flows.
As dawn awakens, bring it near,
In the heart, keep the dreams dear.

The Enigmas of Celestial Gardens

In gardens where the twilight sings,
Whispers weave with fragile wings.
Moonlit petals shimmer bright,
Unfolding secrets of the night.

Among the leaves, the shadows play,
Ancient magic leads the way.
Glistening dew like stars above,
Embracing all with silent love.

Each bloom a tale of joy or woe,
Carried softly by the flow.
Winding paths in twilight's glow,
Guide the lost hearts to and fro.

With every step, the secrets bloom,
Awakening a whispered tune.
In this realm both strange and bright,
Nature hums beneath the night.

The gardens pulse with life untamed,
A dance of magic, wild and famed.
In every corner, the unseen waits,
Holding truths to open gates.

Where Magic Blooms and Creatures Roam

In meadows where the wild things play,
Colors burst in bright array.
Laughter lingers on the breeze,
As sunlight dances through the trees.

Creatures weave through emerald grass,
In shadows deep, the moments pass.
Every step a spell is cast,
In a world where dreams hold fast.

Fanciful fables take their flight,
Underneath the stars so bright.
The moonlight drapes like silver lace,
On serene faces, full of grace.

Where every whisper hints at lore,
And magic opens hidden doors.
The creatures know the tales unsaid,
In a land where hearts can tread.

Beneath the sky of endless hues,
Adventures spark with gentle clues.
Here in this realm, wonder unfolds,
As timeless stories weave like gold.

Celestial Rhythms in Nature's Embrace

In the hush of dawn's first light,
Nature stirs, a wondrous sight.
The sun's warm kiss, the morning dew,
All in tune, a world anew.

The rustling leaves, a gentle song,
Calling creatures, where they belong.
Through branches high, a breeze does sail,
Carrying secrets of the vale.

In harmony, the rivers flow,
Reflecting skies in softest glow.
Mountains stand, both firm and proud,
Guardians etched in misty shroud.

Each star a note in night's refrain,
Echoing softly, sweetly plain.
Celestial rhythms, wild and free,
Guide the whispers of the trees.

Embrace the stillness, feel the grace,
In nature's heart, we find our place.
With every pulse, a story arcs,
In the whispers of the larks.

The Dance of Colors in Mythical Groves

In the glade where dreams converge,
Colors swirl, a vibrant surge.
Petals twirl, in soft ballet,
Nature's magic on display.

Golden rays through branches twine,
Kissing blossoms, pure divine.
A symphony of shades unite,
In every corner, pure delight.

With every step, a new surprise,
Hidden paths before our eyes.
The playful sprites, in frolic there,
Whirling laughter fills the air.

Beneath the stars, a canvas vast,
Where colors dance, the die is cast.
Each flicker bright, a fleeting trace,
Within this enchanted space.

As twilight drapes the world in gold,
Timeless stories come retold.
In these groves where wonders thrive,
Colors pulse, and dreams come alive.

Magic in the Breath of Blossoms

In the garden where dreams softly bloom,
Whispers of magic lift the gloom.
Colors sparkle in the morning dew,
Each petal tells tales, both old and new.

Butterflies flutter, a delicate dance,
With every flutter, a fleeting chance.
Honeybees hum, busy at their art,
Collecting sweet nectar, a labor of heart.

Moonlit petals gleam under the stars,
In the night's embrace, they heal our scars.
A spell of beauty, woven by night,
In the breath of blossoms, hearts take flight.

Magic whispers in the breeze,
Encircling dreams like shimmering trees.
Feel the enchantment, let it unfold,
In the breath of blossoms, we find our gold.

Time stands still, within this space,
Nature's magic, a gentle embrace.
In each delicate fold, a story lies,
Under the watchful, twinkling skies.

The Dance of Light Among the Glades

Sunlight dapples through leaves so green,
In the glades where magic is seen.
Shadows twist, a playful game,
Guided by whispers, calling your name.

Each step on moss is soft and light,
A symphony soaring, nature's delight.
Waves of laughter through branches sway,
In the dance of light, we dream away.

Fairy tales linger where the ferns bend,
Secrets and stories around each bend.
Golden rays weave through the tall trees,
In the glade's embrace, time flows with ease.

As twilight descends, the colors blend,
Mystical melodies begin to send.
In the calm of dusk, a promise remains,
The dance of light, through joy and pains.

Stars peek shyly from dusk's soft haze,
Guiding the way through a dreamy maze.
In the glades, where wonders thrive,
In the dance of light, we feel alive.

Impressions of Wonder in Petal Shades

A canvas brushed with splashes bright,
Petals unfurl in morning light.
Every hue holds a story told,
In the garden of dreams, both vivid and bold.

Fragrant whispers float in the air,
Tales of wonder, a soft affair.
Every blossom a fleeting glance,
An impression of beauty, a whimsical dance.

With the breeze, they twirl and sway,
In a waltz of colors, they softly play.
Mingling together, each shade found,
On the palette of nature, pure joy unbound.

When twilight wraps the world in grace,
Shadows lengthen at a gentle pace.
In the twilight's glow, a secret waits,
The impressions of wonder that life creates.

Under the stars, whispers entice,
In the cool of night, the heart feels nice.
With every petal, a memory stays,
In the impressions of wonder, life sways.

Echoes of Grace in Enchanted Woods

In the depths of woods where silence sings,
Echoes of grace on ethereal wings.
Glimmers of light in a world of dreams,
Whispering secrets in silver streams.

Trees stand tall, guardians of lore,
Holding the whispers of days before.
Each rustle of leaves tells tales so deep,
In the heart of the woods, the magic sleeps.

Footsteps soft on the forest floor,
A journey begins, forevermore.
Each shadow dances, a gentle embrace,
In the echoes of grace, we find our place.

As twilight flows like a tender sigh,
Moonbeams paint dreams in the evening sky.
Nature's canvas, a tapestry spun,
In the enchanted woods, our souls are one.

With each heartbeat, the spirit flies,
In the silent symphony, life never dies.
Echoes of grace linger all around,
In the heart of the woods, pure magic is found.

A Dance of Light in Meadow Dreams

In the meadow, where sunbeams play,
Tiny fairies twirl and sway,
Petals whisper with secrets bright,
In the dance of light, pure delight.

Butterflies flit on gentle breeze,
With laughter that puts hearts at ease,
The grass a carpet, emerald sheen,
In this realm where all is keen.

Golden glow as the dusk draws near,
Softly echoing, songbirds cheer,
Stars awaken, a twinkling choir,
Beneath their gaze, dreams never tire.

Moonlight bathes the world in grace,
Every shadow finds its place,
In the meadow's tranquil heart,
Magic woven into each part.

With every step, a tale unfolds,
Adventures waiting, bright as gold,
In the twilight's tender weave,
A dance of light, we dare believe.

The Color of Fantasy in Nature's Embrace

In the forest, colors bloom,
Every shade dispels the gloom,
Violet whispers, emerald calls,
Nature's canvas, where magic sprawls.

Rivers shimmer like molten gold,
Stories of legends long retold,
Branches weave tales through the air,
In a world of wonder, bright and rare.

Petals glow with morning's kiss,
Filling the heart with purest bliss,
Crimson, azure, and sunset's hue,
In nature's embrace, dreams come true.

Rainbows bridge the skies so high,
Painting whispers in the sky,
As evening paints its evening charms,
With twilight's brush and softest arms.

Each season brings a wondrous show,
Where fantasy and nature grow,
A tapestry, ever so bold,
In colors of stories yet untold.

Whimsical Journeys Through Floral Dreams

In gardens lush, where dreams take root,
Mice and bunnies dance, so astute,
Through blossoms bright, the journey sways,
In whimsical trails, where laughter plays.

The daffodils nod with gentle grace,
Inviting all to join the race,
Through lavender fields and roses fair,
A joyous quest in fragrant air.

Bubbles of laughter, like petals fly,
Painting the clouds in a cerulean sky,
Every footstep tells a tale,
Whispers of magic in the veil.

The whispers of bees, a gentle hum,
Every flower beckons, come, come!
With each flutter, the spirits ensue,
In a realm where dreams feel true.

Adventurers small with hearts ablaze,
Through floral dreams, their spirits blaze,
In a world where wonders gleam,
On whimsical journeys, let them dream.

The Elegy of Fantastical Blooms

Beneath the boughs where shadows linger,
Lies the tale of a delicate finger,
Tracing the petals, soft and bright,
In the elegy of blossoms, pure delight.

Faded memories of blooms long gone,
Whispered promises carried on,
In twilight's glow, a haunting song,
Of fantastical blooms that once thronged.

The air is thick with stories old,
Of love and loss both brave and bold,
Each flower a prism, colors bleed,
A tapestry of dreams and need.

With every whisper, they fade away,
Yet in our hearts, they choose to stay,
For every petal that has flown,
Leaves a mark, a love that's grown.

In the silence, a promise stirs,
As nature sings her softest purrs,
The elegy of blooms sings true,
A testament of life anew.

Luminous Blossoms Under Twilight Enchantment

In gardens where shadows gently creep,
Luminous blossoms, secrets to keep.
Their petals shimmer, kissed by the night,
Whispers of magic, a delicate sight.

Beneath the veil of a starry sky,
Each flower sings, inviting a sigh.
Glowing softly, with a mystical hue,
Promises woven of dreams made anew.

Encased in twilight, where moments blend,
Fates intertwine, as wonders extend.
The breeze carries tales of ages gone,
Through flowered paths that beckon at dawn.

Roots entwined, each story unfolds,
In the heart of the night, a mystery holds.
With every petal that dances with grace,
The world feels lighter in this sacred place.

So linger, dear dreamer, let shadows glide,
Amongst the blossoms, let your heart bide.
For under twilight's enchanting embrace,
True magic lives in each sacred space.

The Saga of Starlit Petals and Creatures

In fields where starlit petals bloom bright,
Creatures gather in the cool, gentle night.
A tale unfolds in whispers and sighs,
As shadows waltz 'neath the watchful skies.

Fireflies dance 'round the blush of a rose,
Each flicker a story that softly glows.
The moon, a guardian, peeks through the trees,
On petals of magic that sway in the breeze.

With every rustle, a promise is shared,
A saga of friendship, tenderly cared.
From delicate wings to whispers of lore,
Nature unveils what her heart has in store.

In the quiet folds of the night's embrace,
Countless journeys await to take place.
So heed the soft murmurs, let them unfurl,
For every petal tells tales of the world.

And as dawn approaches, with golden light,
The saga continues, day turns to night.
Though starlit blooms fade with the rise of the sun,
The laughter of creatures will never be done.

Where Mysteries Blossom in Moonlight

Where mysteries blossom in moon's gentle rays,
In gardens enchanted, where magic decays.
Each petal a secret, each leaf a refrain,
Comforting whispers of joy and of pain.

The nightingale sings of the stories untold,
Of dreams that lie hidden, and hearts made of gold.
In the stillness of midnight, the world seems to pause,
As the sages of old ponder nature's laws.

Like stardust adrift in a shimmering sea,
Bound by the threads of what is and to be.
With each gentle bloom, a new promise grows,
Woven in shadows, where mystery flows.

Through thickets and thorns, a light softly glows,
Leading the seekers where twilight wind blows.
In the heart of the night, where the unknown is found,
True magic awakens, profound yet unbound.

So venture, bright seeker, into the unknown,
Where moonlight reveals what's so rarely shown.
For in every blossom, a tale waits to sprout,
In the embrace of the night, let your spirit break out.

Floral Echoes Amidst Celestial Whispers

In fields where floral echoes softly call,
Celestial whispers weave through the thrall.
Each petal resounds with the song of the stars,
Telling of journeys to Venus and Mars.

A tapestry spun with threads of the night,
Where flowers reach for the moon's tender light.
The air is alive with a rhythmic refrain,
An anthem of beauty brought forth in the rain.

With colors that dance in the warm evening breeze,
Nature's serenade puts the heart at ease.
As fireflies paint secrets upon the dark sky,
Each flicker a promise, each glow not a lie.

Time slows in the moment, where silence is art,
As blossoms whisper all they hold in their heart.
The universe listens, wrapped in delight,
To floral adventures that conquer the night.

So wander through gardens where echoes enclose,
In the hushed, sacred spaces where wonder still grows.
For every flower whispers a tale of the night,
In celestial chambers, where dreams take flight.

Dreams Painted with Floral Hues

In a meadow where wildflowers sway,
Petals whisper secrets of the day.
The sun dips low, casting a glow,
Each bloom a tale that longs to show.

Dreams, like blossoms, rise to the skies,
With colors vibrant, they mesmerize.
A canvas bright, the artist's delight,
Imagination takes its flight.

Beneath the arch of a leafy bower,
Thoughts entwined with each passing hour.
Nature's brush, so deft and kind,
Paints the wonders of the mind.

Twilight sings, a gentle breeze,
Carrying hopes like autumn leaves.
In twilight's embrace, they twirl and dance,
Finding magic in every chance.

A tapestry woven with care and grace,
In floral hues, we find our place.
As dreams unfold in sweet perfume,
A world awakens, free to bloom.

Harmonies in the Starlit Garden

Underneath the silver glow,
Stars perform a quiet show.
In the garden, shadows sway,
Night birds sing, the heart's bouquet.

Petals bloom, a soft parade,
In the stillness, whispers made.
Each note dances on the air,
In this realm of beauty rare.

With every twinkle, every gleam,
Nature weaves a tender dream.
The nightingale, her song so sweet,
Guides the flowers to their beat.

Wandering through this ethereal light,
Lost in wonder, pure delight.
A serenade of every hue,
In the garden, dreams come true.

As the dawn begins to peep,
Secrets of the night we keep.
In the heart of the starlit land,
Harmonies held in nature's hand.

Enchanted Flora and Ethereal Beasts

In forests deep, where shadows play,
Flora dances, light and spray.
Ethereal beasts roam wild and free,
Guardians of the tranquility.

Petals whisper to the trees,
Stories carried by the breeze.
Moonlight bathes the ancient wood,
In nature's heart, the magic stood.

Mushrooms glow with a mystic light,
Creatures hidden, shy from sight.
With every footstep, tales unfold,
Of enchantments woven, brave and bold.

Gentle creatures weave a dream,
In the moonlit night's silver beam.
Here, the boundary fades from view,
Where magic lives in every hue.

Intertwined with every breath,
Flora sings of life and death.
In this realm, where wonders churn,
Hearts awaken, and spirits yearn.

Where Moonlight Dances with Wildflowers

In a glade where the shadows sigh,
Moonlight spills from the velvet sky.
Wildflowers sway in a tender trance,
Each petal captures the night's romance.

Crickets sing a lullaby clear,
Dancing dreams now drawing near.
The night unfolds its soft embrace,
Enchanting moments, time and space.

Winds whisper secrets through the leaves,
In this haven, all heart believes.
Every shadow holds a tale,
Of fleeting joy, and love's sweet trail.

Illuminated by the moon's soft gaze,
The garden bursts into a magical haze.
Wildflowers bloom in the silver glow,
Where time stands still, and dreams can grow.

Together, they weave a fragrant delight,
As moonlight dances into the night.
In the stillness, with nature entwined,
We find the beauty that love designed.

A Tapestry of Fragrance and Light

In gardens where the sunlight spills,
The daisies dance on gentle hills.
A whisper flows through fragrant air,
A tapestry of scents laid bare.

The roses blush, with petals bright,
Their sweet perfume, a pure delight.
In twilight's glow, the shadows play,
As twilight bids the sun good day.

While jasmine twines 'round ancient trees,
The evening hums with softest breeze.
In every bloom, a story weaves,
Of dreams and hopes, the heart believes.

Through violets and lilacs fair,
The fragrance lingers, light as air.
A symphony of hues so bold,
In every petal, tales unfold.

So let us wander, hand in hand,
Through fragrant fields, a magic land.
Where every scent, a memory,
In light's embrace, we wander free.

Ethereal Equines in Blooming Fields

In fields of gold, where wildflowers sway,
Ethereal equines come out to play.
With manes that glimmer like morning dew,
They dance in joy, beneath skies so blue.

Their hooves are whispers on the breeze,
As they prance lightly among the trees.
Each step a grace, each leap a flight,
Beneath the sun, they glow so bright.

From distant valleys, a song resounds,
Magic bound in the beauty found.
With every neigh, a tale takes form,
In nature's arms, they are reborn.

Through fragrant clover, they make their way,
Chasing sunbeams that dance and sway.
In laughter's echo, they find their path,
Eternal joy, in nature's bath.

As twilight hushes the world around,
These creatures gather, magic unbound.
With stars as witnesses, they take flight,
Ethereal dreams melt into night.

Fragrant Fables Beneath Twinkling Stars

Beneath the stars, where shadows twirl,
Fragrant fables of dusk unfurl.
With every breeze, a tale is spun,
Of moonlit hearts and love begun.

The garden hums with secret sighs,
As silver beams paint velvet skies.
Through roses red and violets blue,
Whispers of magic linger too.

While owls compose their midnight prose,
And stars become the tales they chose.
In every scent, a legend breathes,
Of ancient dreams that twilight weaves.

The jasmine blooms with stories sweet,
As crickets play a rhythmic beat.
Each fragrance holds a memory dear,
A moment captured, crystal clear.

So wrap your heart in fragrant night,
And let the fables take their flight.
For in the dark, our dreams ignite,
Beneath the stars, all feels just right.

Petal-Crowned Creatures of Wonder

In twilight's glow, where dreams awake,
Petal-crowned creatures dance and shake.
With glimmering eyes, they flit and glide,
Through blossoms blooming, side by side.

With wings of silk, they weave through air,
Their laughter light, a joyful flare.
Among the petals, secrets bloom,
In every shade, dispelling gloom.

As moonbeams kiss the floral ground,
These wondrous beings whirl around.
Each creature holds a story bright,
A tale of love that conquers night.

In meadows lush, where shadows dance,
They skip in time, a fleeting chance.
With every twirl, the magic sings,
Of hopes that soar on whispered wings.

So let us join their merry throng,
In vibrant fields, where we belong.
With hearts ablaze in joy and cheer,
The petal-crowned will always near.

A Melody of Fantastical Blossoms

In gardens where magic whispers low,
Petals glimmer with an inner glow.
Each hue sings tales of joy and grace,
A vibrant dance, a fleeting chase.

Beneath the boughs where fairies play,
Soft voices weave the light of day.
With every breeze, the blossoms sway,
Creating tunes that gently stay.

Butterflies flit in joyful flight,
Painting the air with colors bright.
They join the song, the sweetest sound,
In this enchanted, hallowed ground.

The sunbeams kiss the flowers' bloom,
Casting aside the shades of gloom.
In harmony, they sing and sway,
As twilight brings the end of day.

As night descends and stars take flight,
The blossoms whisper soft goodnight.
In dreams, their melody will soar,
A wondrous tune forevermore.

Soft Fragrances in a Celestial Glade

In the heart of a glade, where whispers blend,
Lies a fragrant path that twists and bends.
Moonflowers bloom in the silver light,
Their petals shimmering, pure and white.

Gentle breezes weave a sweet refrain,
Easing the world of worry and pain.
Each breath a gift, with petals so rare,
Soft fragrances fill the tranquil air.

Fireflies dance in a rhythmic trance,
Guiding the eye with a flickering glance.
They spark the night with their tiny beams,
As dreams unfold in shimmering themes.

The nightingale sings of love and fate,
Her song a lullaby, quiet and great.
Each note drifts softly, a soothing touch,
Inviting all hearts to feel so much.

And when the dawn breaks through the trees,
The glade awakens with morning's breeze.
Whispers of magic remain in the air,
As celestial secrets, we gently share.

The Dance of Unicorns and Petal Dreams

In a meadow where the sunbeams play,
Unicorns prance in a joyful sway.
Their hooves create a melodious sound,
While petals flutter softly to the ground.

With flowing manes that glisten like dew,
They twirl beneath skies of azure hue.
Wings of laughter ripple in the air,
As dreams weave tales beyond compare.

Bright rainbows arch in a painted sky,
Each arc a promise, a gentle sigh.
In this realm where magic reigns supreme,
Every heart takes flight on a seraph's dream.

Petal dreams dance like whispers of night,
Carried on breezes, soft and light.
They twine with magic in every beam,
Creating a tapestry of each dream.

So let your spirit soar in delight,
Join with the unicorns, take flight.
In the dance of dreams, our souls will gleam,
Together we cultivate hope's sweet theme.

Lullabies in the Land of Blooming Dreams

In the land where dreams begin to flow,
Gentle lullabies in twilight glow.
Clouds of cotton candy softly drift,
Cradling wishes as a precious gift.

Beneath the stars that twinkle bright,
Night flowers bloom in soft moonlight.
Their fragrances weave a serene spell,
Inviting all to a sweet farewell.

The brook hums softly, a whispered tune,
Beneath the watchful gaze of the moon.
It dances over stones worn smooth and grey,
Carrying dreams as they gently sway.

In this haven where time stands still,
Laughter and love, an unbroken thrill.
With every breath, the magic springs,
As the heart learns the joy that dreaming brings.

So close your eyes, let the night unfold,
In stories waiting to be told.
In the land of dreams, where magic gleams,
The lullabies flow like enchanted streams.

Whimsy in the Twilight Blossom Grove

In twilight's glow, where blossoms dance,
Beneath the stars, they sway and prance.
The air is steeped in sweet delight,
With whispers soft, the dreams take flight.

A brook giggles, weaving through,
Its laughter paints the night anew.
While fireflies twinkle, play their game,
Each flicker hints of joy untamed.

The trees wear cloaks of shimmering lace,
Embracing night's soft, warm embrace.
And faeries spin tales on sighing winds,
Where magic lingers, and hope rescinds.

Each petal tells a story bright,
Of secret worlds in the silver light.
A gentle breeze brings softest sighs,
As time dissolves, and silence flies.

In the grove where whimsy reigns,
Each heart released from weary chains.
With every bloom, a promise made,
In twilight's bloom, all worries fade.

Forest of the Forgotten Unicorn

In shadows deep, where whispers dwell,
A forest holds its ancient spell.
Beneath the boughs, in muted light,
A hooved heart beats, both fierce and bright.

Through tangled brambles, legends creep,
Of creatures lost in silent sleep.
With silver mane and eyes aglow,
The unicorn dances, longing to show.

Forgotten paths of dreams untold,
Where time retreats, and love grows bold.
Amidst the ferns and mossy beds,
The echoes of the past are fed.

In twilight's breath, she calls anew,
To hearts that seek the pure and true.
With gentle grace, she roams the glade,
In every shimmer, a promise made.

The forest whispers secrets rare,
Of love entwined in moonlit air.
And in each glimmer, fate entwines,
As magic sparks in whispered signs.

Moonlit Secrets in Floral Realms

Beneath the moon, the flowers sigh,
Unfolding petals to the sky.
Each bloom a promise, soft and sweet,
In secrets held, the worlds entreat.

A garden glows with silver sheen,
Where shadows dance in shades of green.
The nightingale sings soft and low,
Echoes of dreams in gentle flow.

In hidden nooks, the faeries play,
Crafting wishes, night and day.
With stardust dreams and laughter bright,
They weave the magic of the night.

The air is rich with fragrant tales,
Of whispered hopes on twilight trails.
Each flourishing bud a story spun,
In moonlit realms where love is won.

In floral realms, where shadows blend,
The heart's true journey finds its end.
To dance beneath the starry dome,
In whispered dreams, we find our home.

A Tapestry of Color and Wonder

In fields where colors burst and weave,
A tapestry made for hearts to believe.
With golden threads of sun's embrace,
And silvery stars that twinkle in space.

Each petal holds a vibrant dream,
Flowing forth like a gentle stream.
From azure skies to emerald blades,
In nature's palette, joy cascades.

The daisies nod in playful cheer,
While butterflies drift ever near.
A canvas painted by the dawn,
Where beauty wakes with every yawn.

In whispered winds, a tale unfolds,
Of love and laughter, dreams retold.
Through every shade, a story flows,
In color's dance, the wonder grows.

So let your spirit boldly soar,
To find the magic at the core.
In this grand tapestry we find,
A world of wonder, intertwined.

The Harmony of Flora and Fable

In fields where daisies dance and sway,
Their whispered tales unfold each day.
With colors bright, the petals sing,
A symphony of life in spring.

The ancient trees stand wise and tall,
Guardians of secrets, known to all.
Their roots entwined with stories old,
From every bud, a truth unfolds.

Beneath the arch of twilight's glow,
The hidden paths where fairies go.
A melody of laughter bright,
In shadows deep, they find their light.

As twilight weaves her velvet lace,
The flora twirls in magical grace.
Each blossom tells a tale of yore,
Of fables spun on nature's floor.

So wander forth through lands untold,
Where flora's whispers dare be bold.
Embrace the harmony of night,
In every leaf, find pure delight.

Twilight Whispers in the Unicorn Grove

In a grove where shadows softly croon,
And silvered light enchants the moon,
The unicorns with elegance tread,
In twilight's embrace, their spirits led.

Their manes, a cascade of starlit threads,
As night descends, the magic spreads.
With every step, enchantments wake,
In dreams of wonder, hearts do quake.

Fluttering whispers in the air,
The scent of blossoms, wondrous and rare.
Where wishes linger on a breeze,
And timeless moments seek to please.

The moonlit glade, a sacred space,
Where hope and dreams find soft embrace.
In gentle reverie, hearts align,
With every heartbeat, stars entwine.

Through silver hues and shadows deep,
The unicorns their secrets keep.
In every rustle, magic flows,
In twilight's arms, true wonder grows.

Petals and Dreams Under a Starlit Sky

Beneath the vast, enchanting night,
Where stardust sparkles, pure delight,
The flowers bloom in colors bright,
As dreams take flight in soft moonlight.

Each petal holds a whispered song,
In shifting shadows, they belong.
The breeze carries tales of yore,
Of hopes and dreams that yearn for more.

A tapestry of light unfurls,
As evening dances, softly twirls.
With every twinkle, wishes soar,
In starlit realms, we seek to explore.

Crickets serenade the gentle night,
While fireflies weave their glowing light.
In every heartbeat, magic sways,
A reminder of the wondrous days.

Underneath this cosmic dome,
Where every petal finds its home,
Embrace the dreams that softly sigh,
In harmony with the starlit sky.

Serene Colors of Fantastical Fables

In lands where colors freely blend,
Where stories weave and never end.
With every hue, a tale ignites,
In fantastical fables, pure delights.

The emerald fields, a canvas wide,
With sapphire skies that stretch and glide.
Golden sunbeams kiss the earth,
As laughter echoes, giving birth.

Each blossom whispers secrets dear,
As memories drift, both far and near.
Through vibrant meadows, tales unfold,
Of heroes brave and dreams of gold.

In twilight's embrace, soft colors sway,
As evening hues melt into gray.
With every shade, a story flows,
In serene colors, magic grows.

So journey on through realms of dreams,
Where every fable softly gleams.
In hearts alive, the colors play,
A symphony of night and day.

Elysian Fields of Myth and Blossom

In fields where ancient stories weave,
The daisies dance in sunlight's weave.
Each petal holds a whispered tale,
Of heroes bold who never fail.

Beneath the boughs of elder trees,
The evening hums with gentle breeze.
A tapestry of dreams unfurled,
In this enchanted, magical world.

The violets speak in shades of blue,
While fragrant roses blush anew.
Soft melodies from brooks nearby,
Join in the chorus of the sky.

Where moonbeams kiss the grassy knoll,
And fireflies take their evening stroll.
A lullaby to soothe the night,
By starlit paths and silver light.

So wander here with heart aglow,
In Elysium where dreams will flow.
For every moment blossoms sweet,
In myth and bloom, our lives complete.

Celestial Trails of Flowery Whispers

Upon the sky in twilight's grace,
Celestial trails softly embrace.
With whispers carried on the breeze,
The flowers bloom with such sweet ease.

Petals drift like dreams set free,
In colors bright for all to see.
Each blossom tells a story spun,
Of silver moons and golden sun.

As stars awaken, soft and bright,
They twinkle down with gentle light.
In fragrant gardens, shadows play,
While night unveils its grand ballet.

The lilacs laugh, the lilies sigh,
With every note, the nightbirds fly.
A symphony of scents arise,
Transforming earth beneath the skies.

So lose yourself in this embrace,
Of flowered dreams and cosmic space.
For in each whisper, magic glows,
On celestial paths where wonder flows.

A Symphony of Petals and Starry Nights

In gardens where the night unfolds,
A symphony of petals golds.
The moonlight sprinkles silver seeds,
And nature hums, fulfilling needs.

Each flower sways to evening's tune,
Beneath the watchful, glowing moon.
The crickets play their soft refrain,
While dreams and blooms begin to reign.

A melody of scent and sight,
Dances upon the edge of night.
Tulips sing beneath the stars,
While violets cradle whispered bars.

The roses blush in twilight's glow,
As breezes rustle soft and low.
In harmony, the night enchants,
With nature's rhythm, hearts will dance.

So join the song, let spirits soar,
In fields of dreams forevermore.
For every petal's gentle sway,
Is life and love in grand display.

Veils of Petals and Enchanted Tales

Beneath the arch of willow trees,
Veils of petals float on the breeze.
Each layer holds a story's thread,
Of love and magic, softly said.

The daffodils in sunlight gleam,
Like golden notes of nature's dream.
In every bloom, a secret kept,
Of whispered vows and sorrows wept.

Through tangled paths of fragrant hues,
The lilting wind reveals its muse.
In every sigh, a tale is spun,
Of battles lost and victories won.

A carpet woven of the night,
Where shadows dance in ghostly light.
Amidst the petals, stories roam,
In every heart, they find a home.

So wander deep where magic trails,
In veils of petals and glowing tales.
For in this realm of dreams so bright,
We find our truth in endless light.

Nature's Essence in a Magical Landscape

In the heart of a grove so deep,
Where secrets of nature quietly sleep,
Whispers of leaves dance on the breeze,
Echoing tales of ancient trees.

Streams of silver weave through the lands,
Carrying dreams in their gentle hands,
Rustling flowers in vibrant hues,
Painting the world with nature's muse.

Mountains rise like giants in grace,
Beneath the sky's soft, azure face,
Misty mornings awaken the day,
Inviting magic to come out and play.

Petals glisten with dew's caress,
Holding the magic in their finesse,
As sunlight spills gold upon the ground,
Transforming silence into a sound.

Each moment here is a treasure untold,
Nature's essence in beauty so bold,
Where every sigh and every glance,
Is a step into a wondrous dance.

Starlit Tales of Serene Blooms

Under the blanket of twilight's grace,
Soft blooms whisper in a starry place,
Moonlight kisses each petal's hue,
In a garden where dreams come true.

Crickets sing in a melodic choir,
As vibrant blooms reach higher and higher,
With fragrance sweet as an evening song,
In this realm where all souls belong.

Gentle breezes carry tales of bliss,
Of starlit romances sealed with a kiss,
In shadows where the soft night glows,
Magic in each delicate rose.

As the world around drifts into night,
Serene blooms bask in the silver light,
Each flower a beacon of hope and peace,
In the garden where troubles cease.

With every star twinkling above,
Nature sings a lullaby of love,
Amongst the petals, secrets unfold,
In starlit tales of serenity told.

The Enchantment of Floral Whispers

In the meadow where flowers sway,
Whispers of color dance and play,
With each petal a story to share,
Enchantment lingers in the air.

Daisies nod in a gentle breeze,
While violets bend with elegant ease,
Sunflowers turn to the golden sun,
In this land where all hearts are one.

With dewdrops clinging like pearls on silk,
Nature's canvas, smooth as milk,
Wildflowers laugh with the grace of spring,
In their presence, the world takes wing.

Petals unfurl secrets of light,
Drawing the stars into the night,
Fragrant breezes whisper and curl,
Enchanting the heart in a floral swirl.

Amidst the blooms, magic abounds,
In each soft rustle, the universe sounds,
With every step, a wish can soar,
In whispers of nature, forevermore.

Celestial Scent of Dreams Unfurled

In gardens where the cosmos align,
Celestial scents weave a design,
With fragrant breezes that softly blend,
Echoes of dreams that never end.

Petals blush in the dawn's embrace,
Capturing light with exquisite grace,
A tapestry woven of hopes and dreams,
Glowing softly in sunlit beams.

As night descends, stars begin to gleam,
Nurturing visions like a gentle dream,
Each bloom opens its heart to the sky,
Letting sweet scents of longing fly.

In the quiet, beauty unfolds,
Secrets of nature in whispers told,
Each fragrance holds a promise bright,
In the celestial dance of day and night.

So wander through this enchanted land,
Where dreams and blossoms go hand in hand,
With each step, let your spirit twirl,
In the celestial scent of dreams unfurled.

Moonlit Meadows and Fantastical Spirits

In moonlit meadows where shadows dance,
Beneath the gaze of stars that prance,
Whispers of fairies in gentle light,
Twinkling secrets on this dreamy night.

A brook babbles tales of ancient lore,
While silver beams glide o'er the forest floor,
Creatures of magic weave through the trees,
In a world where wonder is carried by the breeze.

Fields of clover wrapped in dew,
Dance with spirits, old and new,
Each petal soft, a story to tell,
Of realms beyond where dreamers dwell.

Their laughter echoes, a melodic tune,
As they frolic beneath the glowing moon,
In moonlit meadows, the night unfolds,
A tapestry woven with threads of gold.

So linger a while in this enchanted space,
Where dreams and reality momentarily embrace,
For in these meadows, with hearts so free,
Life becomes art, as we take to the lea.

The Elegance of Mystical Gardens

In gardens where the lilies sway,
Whispers of magic linger and play,
Petals unfurl in a soft ballet,
Sharing secrets at the break of day.

Gossamer webs catch the morning dew,
While sunbeams dance, in hues so blue,
With fragrance of blooms that rise and twirl,
In this retreat where wonders unfurl.

Amidst the paths of emerald green,
Where dreams of faeries are often seen,
Their laughter blooms in the lilac shade,
As shadows waltz where magic is laid.

Time flows gently in this sacred space,
Each blossom a smile, each leaf a grace,
A chorus of colors, vivid and bright,
In the elegance of gardens, pure delight.

So wander freely, let your spirit soar,
In these mystical gardens, forevermore,
For happiness hides in each fragrant breath,
In nature's embrace, we conquer death.

Sylvan Dreams and Floral Whispers

In sylvan dreams where whispers bloom,
Each sigh of wind dispels the gloom,
Daisies twirl in a sunlit twine,
As shadows dance in a gentle line.

Winding paths weave through the trees,
With melodies caressed by the breeze,
Floral whispers echo, soft and sweet,
In a realm where every heart skips a beat.

Beneath the ferns, old tales reside,
Of magic, love, and the world's wide ride,
With every color, a story is spun,
In this haven where all fears are done.

Glimmers of sunlight pierce the green,
Painting dreams where we've always been,
With each petal a promise, a wish afloat,
In sylvan embrace, our spirits emote.

So linger here where the wild things grow,
In the arms of nature, let your heart glow,
For sylvan dreams are a treasure divine,
Where moments of magic eternally shine.

Starlit Paths Through Floral Wonderland

On starlit paths where shadows melt,
Stories of wonder and dreams are felt,
Each step a soft echo in twilight's embrace,
Leading us deeper into this magical space.

Under the canopy of twinkling spheres,
Where silence sings and heartache clears,
Floral wonderlands beckon with grace,
Inviting wanderers to linger and chase.

Moonflowers bloom in the velvet night,
Emitting whispers of soft, pure light,
With every petal, a wish made clear,
In this enchanting realm, there's nothing to fear.

The fragrance of jasmine, sweet on the air,
Twirls in the starlight, a delicate snare,
Enchanting the souls who dare to believe,
In the magic of night, we learn to perceive.

So stroll through the flowers, let your heart soar,
On starlit paths, find what you adore,
For in this wonderland, dreams come alive,
In dreams, we shall wander, in dreams, we shall thrive.